N I C K   F A

A New Day Dawning

Personal
meditations
for Advent
and Christmas

Kevin
Mayhew

First published in 2001 by
KEVIN MAYHEW LTD
Buxhall, Stowmarket, Suffolk IP14 3BW
Email: info@kevinmayhewltd.com

9 8 7 6 5 4 3 2 1 0

ISBN 1 84003 806 3
Catalogue No 1500458

Cover design by Jonathan Stroulger
Edited by Katherine Laidler
Typesetting by Richard Weaver

Printed and bound in Great Britain

Contents

Introduction

A new day dawning – it's a nice picture, isn't it, conjuring up scenes of the sun slowly peeping over the horizon, bathing the world in warmth and light? It is a time that ushers in another day, full of promise and opportunity, and so, unsurprisingly, dawn has long spoken to people of new beginnings, a fresh start. That, at least, is the theory. In practice, one day can be much like another, life settling into a regular pattern repeated week in, week out. Can we meaningfully talk of experiencing a new dawn? The answer, according to the gospel, is an emphatic 'yes', and Advent and Christmas remind us why, for they speak of the greatest new dawn of all.

'The sun will rise over us from heaven,' says Zechariah, in the gospel of Luke (1:78-79) 'to shine on those sitting in darkness and in the shadow of death; to guide our feet into the way of peace.' His words capture something of the wonder, joy and hope associated with the coming of Christ. Here was one who would bring joy where there was sorrow, hope where there was despair, love where there was hatred, and peace where there was division; not just a fresh chapter in history but also the possibility of a similar renewal in every human heart comparable to the rising of the sun; a new dawn!

This collection of prayers, meditations and reflections, taken from a number of my earlier books, is concerned with that new dawn brought about by the birth of Christ. It explores what his coming meant for those directly touched by it, and what it means for us today. Intended as a tool for personal devotion, it looks both at the events of Bethlehem and at his coming again in our lives today. It starts, though, before that, at the dawn of human history, and moves on to consider the implications of the promised return of Christ at the end of time – themes that take us to the very heart of Advent. The intention, throughout, is to stimulate reflection; to help you, the reader, enter into the nativity stories in such a way that you see them in a new light. What must it have felt like to be

Zechariah, Mary or Joseph, suddenly confronted with a messenger from God; or one of the shepherds, crowding round the manger, or one of the wise men, at last at the end of your journey, kneeling in homage before the Christ child? What would you have made of it all? How would you have reacted? Most important of all, how would it have changed your life?

We do not know the full story of those involved in the astonishing events of Bethlehem, for we are not told whether they came to faith in Christ. What we do know is that, following in the footsteps of the Apostles, many across the years have found in him a new beginning, a fresh chapter opening up in their lives. They discovered the truth of 'God with us' spoken of in Matthew; of the kingdom within, spoken of in Mark; of good news for all people, spoken of in Luke; of becoming children of God, spoken of in John. They discovered a new day dawning. My hope, in putting together this collection of meditations, is that they may remind us of the new dawn God is able to bring us, today and every day.

Nick Fawcett

1
What have I done?
God

Advent revolves around two key themes – the coming of Christ and his coming again in glory. Yet to understand each of those, there is a vital question we need to ask: Why did he have to come in the first place? To answer that we need to look not to last times, nor to the words of the prophets, nor even to the stable in Bethlehem, but to the dawn of time itself and the purpose of God in creation. According to Genesis, God made humankind in his likeness, his desire that we should share his life and experience his love, but from the start, that loving purpose was frustrated as free will led to sin rearing its ugly head. What should have been creation living in harmony became a broken and divided world. How must God have felt as he looked out at all he had made and saw violence rather than harmony, hatred rather than love, corruption instead of innocence? Was he tempted to abandon the whole exercise, to write off creation as an ill-fated experiment? According to the story of Noah, yes, yet he could not finally bring himself to take such a drastic step – almost, but not quite. Instead, he resolved to redeem the world, to rectify by his grace what we could never put right through our own efforts. What we celebrate at Advent is the decisive step in that process through the coming of Christ; what we look forward to is the consummation of his will when Jesus comes again.

Reading: Genesis 3:1-13

Now the serpent was more crafty than any other wild animal that the Lord God had made. He said to the woman, 'Did God say,

"You shall not eat from any tree in the garden"?' The woman said to the serpent, 'We may eat of the fruit of the trees in the garden; but God said, "You shall not eat of the fruit of the tree that is in the middle of the garden, nor shall you touch it, or you shall die."' But the serpent said to the woman, 'You will not die; for God knows that when you eat of it your eyes will be opened, and you will be like God knowing good and evil.' So when the woman saw that the tree was good for food, and that it was a delight to the eyes, and that the tree was to be desired to make one wise, she took of its fruit and ate; and she also gave some to her husband, who was with her, and he ate.

Then the eyes of both were opened, and they knew that they were naked; and they sewed fig leaves together and made loincloths for themselves. They heard the sound of the Lord God walking in the garden at the time of the evening breeze, and the man and his wife hid themselves from the presence of the Lord among the trees of the garden. But the Lord God called to the man, and said to him, 'Where are you?' He said, 'I heard the sound of you in the garden, and I was afraid, because I was naked; and I hid myself.' He said, 'Who told you that you were naked? Have you eaten from the tree of which I commanded you not to eat?' The man said, 'The woman whom you gave to be with me, she gave me fruit from the tree, and I ate.' Then the Lord God said to the woman, 'What is this that you have done?' The woman said, 'The serpent tricked me, and I ate.'

(The idyllic picture of Eden, soon gives way to one altogether different.)

Genesis 6:5-6

The Lord saw that the wickedness of humankind was great in the earth, and that every inclination of the thoughts of their hearts was only evil continually. And the Lord was sorry that he had made humankind on the earth, and it grieved him to his heart.

Meditation

What have I done?
What *have* I done?
Day after day I look at the world I've made,
    intended to be so beautiful,
    so special,
    and I see hatred,
    violence,
    greed,
    corruption –
    so much that maims and mutilates,
    destroying hope,
    denying life.
Can you imagine what it feels like,
    living with the awfulness of ultimate responsibility,
    and bearing that not just for a fleeting span but for all eternity?
I don't think you can.
But, believe me, whatever pain *you've* endured,
    whatever sorrow or heartbreak,
    it can never touch the agony
    of watching your creation slowly tearing itself apart.
Was it all a mistake?
Some will say so, and I can't blame them.
Yet I had love to give and life to share –
    would it have been any more moral to keep that to myself?
I could, of course, have made you like puppets,
    every thought controlled,
    every action directed,
    but is that what you'd have wanted?–
    unable to think or feel,
    deprived of joy for lack of sorrow,
    love for lack of hate,
    hope for lack of fear,
    pleasure for lack of pain.

Don't tell me I'm not to blame, for it just won't do.
I made you, didn't I? –
    mine the hand that brought you into being –
    so, though the mistakes may be yours, the fault surely is mine.
There will be punishment and justice –
    there has to be –
    yet don't think I've given up on you,
    for, perfect or imperfect, I still love you,
    and I'm going to go on loving for as long as it takes,
    giving my all for you,
    my very life,
    until the broken threads of creation are woven together
    into a glorious new tapestry,
    and we are one, you and I,
    united in paradise,
    now and for ever.

Prayer

God of all,
    I look at the world sometimes –
    at its suffering and sorrow, hurt and heartbreak –
    and I don't understand why you let it happen.
I see evil and injustice, hatred and greed;
    so much that frustrates your will and denies your purpose;
    and I cannot help ask:
    'Where are you in the face of it?'
My mind struggles to take in the great mysteries of life
    for I am a part of your fallen creation.
Yet, though I cannot always make sense of your will,
    I believe that your nature is love,
    and that the time will come when my questions will be answered
    and your purpose revealed.

Until then, help me to live with paradox
    and trust in your eternal promises,
        knowing that every moment of every day you are at work,
        striving to bring creation to perfection.
Through Christ my Lord.
Amen.

2
The people who walked in darkness
Resident of Jerusalem

Few passages of the Old Testament are better known and better loved than the opening verses of Isaiah chapter 9. The idea of a great light shining on those who walked in darkness is a wonderfully evocative picture – the image continuing to resonate with us today – yet how far, if at all, do we believe it can be realised in our own experience? A look at the world around us seems to give little reason to hope; the news headlines, day after day, full of yet more violence, corruption, suffering and goodness knows what else. How far, realistically, can we talk of light shining on us, either now or in the future? Must hope be consigned altogether to another time and kingdom? I've no doubt many felt just that in the years leading up to the coming of Christ. As so often in their history, the Jews found themselves a subject people, smarting under the occupation of the Roman legions. Discontent was rife, and, if the testimony of Malachi is to be believed, injustice and oppression were everywhere. Following a succession of supposed 'Messiahs', many had given up hoping that a Messiah would come, the very idea seeming like a naïve delusion. Yet, of course, in the stable in Bethlehem, God's promised deliverer was born; the one whom the Apostle John was to describe as 'the true light, which enlightens everyone'. That did not mean darkness suddenly disappeared; in fact, for a time, as Jesus hung on the cross, it seemed to have triumphed. Ultimately, however, the light could not be extinguished. We need to hold on to that truth today, confident that, despite appearances, the light shines in the darkness and nothing will overcome it.

Reading: Isaiah 9:2, 6-7

The people who walked in darkness have seen a great light; those who lived in a land of deep darkness – on them light has shined. For a child has been born for us, a son given to us; authority rests upon his shoulders; and he is named Wonderful Counsellor, Mighty God, Everlasting Father, Prince of Peace. His authority shall grow continually, and there shall be endless peace for the throne of David and his kingdom. He will establish and uphold it with justice and with righteousness from this time onward and for evermore. The zeal of the Lord of hosts will do this.

Meditation

'The people who walked in darkness have seen a great light.'
Do you remember those words?
Of course you do – it's hard not to, isn't it?
But do you think they mean anything?
Do you actually believe that things will change,
    that the Messiah will come and finally establish his kingdom?
I used to, once.
I used to read that passage time and again,
    a warm glow stealing over me until I tingled with anticipation,
    convinced that God would soon transform this world of ours.
Any day now, I thought,
    it can't be long –
    surely?
But another day, another month, another year came and went,
    and, with each one, faith lost a little of its sparkle,
    until now the lustre is just about gone,
    no more than a dull gleam left
    where once that confidence shone so brightly.
What happened?
Did I misunderstand something,
    or did the prophet get it wrong,

his vision not the glorious promise I thought it was
but an empty illusory dream?
Believe me, I want to think otherwise,
my spirit still crying out to be proved wrong,
but just look around you,
at the sin,
the suffering,
the sorrow,
the squalor,
and then tell me honestly:
where is God in all this?
Can you see that light he promised?
I can't.
I've waited, as so many have waited before me,
telling myself that evil can't have the last word,
the good must finally triumph,
but there's still no sign,
nothing to give grounds for optimism,
and it's all I can do not to lose heart completely.
Yet I must hope,
somehow, despite it all, I must keep faith,
for if there's really nothing else in this world than what you see,
then God help us!
I may have my doubts,
and it may not be easy,
but so long as there's even the merest spark of faith left,
the tiniest, faintest flicker,
I'm going to go on hoping,
and go on praying,
come, Lord,
come!

Prayer

Gracious God,
    help me to recognise,
    despite everything that seems to belie your love
    and undermine my faith,
    that you are at work in this world,
    reaching out wherever there is darkness
    to bring your help and healing, hope and wholeness.
Teach me to look to Christ, who,
    through the darkness of the cross,
    brought life and light to all,
    and so help me to understand that even when I cannot see it,
    your light continues to shine.
Come again, then, to our world of so much need,
    and may the light of your love shine within me
    and in the hearts of all,
    to the glory of your name.
Amen.

3
Does this sound daft to you?
Isaiah

A vision of the future or sentimental nonsense; a realistic picture of what life might be like or a wistful portrait of what it might have been – what do you make of the words of Isaiah chapter 11? Memorable words they certainly are, but are they simply poetic imagery or prophetic foresight? In terms of this life, at least, both those appraisals contain an element of truth. In recent years we have seen startling moves towards peace in some quarters of the world, yet also there have been unspeakable atrocities and mind-boggling inhumanity. Sadly, for every reason to hope there seems to be still more cause to despair, and, eventually, few of us can avoid disillusionment setting in. We'd like to believe in a world such as the prophet paints – a time of peace and harmony, when violence, discord and hatred will be a thing of the past – but most of us take such claims with a strong pinch of salt. Life, we tell ourselves, is just not like that. Realism rather than the idealism invariably wins the day. Such an attitude is understandable given the lament-able record of human history and the continuing divisions in our world today, yet it cannot finally be acceptable. *We* may abandon the world to its fate – God never will. He will not rest until his will is done and his kingdom established, on earth as it is in heaven. It may seem light years away from the world as we know it today, but we must never lose that vision of what life can become, nor stop working towards it.

Reading: Isaiah 11:1-9

A shoot will spring up from the stump of Jesse and a branch grow from his roots. The spirit of the Lord will rest on him – a spirit of wisdom and understanding, of discernment and might, of knowledge and the fear of the Lord, and he will delight in the fear of the Lord.

He will not judge by appearances, or decide by what his ears hear; but he will justly judge the cause of the poor and even-handedly defend the meek of the earth; he will strike the earth with the rod of his mouth, and by the breath of his lips kill the wicked. He will wear righteousness like a belt round his waist, and girdle his loins with faithfulness.

The wolf will live with the lamb, the leopard lie down with the kid, the calf and the lion and the fatling together, and a little child will lead them. The cow and the bear will graze, and their young lie down together; and the lion will eat straw like the ox. Babies will play over the nest of a cobra, and the weaned child will put its hand in the adder's den. They will not hurt or destroy anywhere on my holy mountain; for the earth will be full of the knowledge of the Lord, as the waters cover the sea.

Meditation

Does this sound daft to you –
    a wolf lying down with a lamb,
    a lion grazing with an ox,
    a child playing happily with a snake?
It does to me, I have to admit it,
    now I've had time to consider the implications.
But it didn't at the time,
    not when the idea first caught hold of me.
You see, I had this picture of a different kind of world,
    a society where barriers are broken down,
        where all the petty disputes that so often divide us
        are a thing of the past.
Imagine it –
    no more violence,
    no more fear,

no more hatred,
no more suffering –
a world at one with itself,
all creatures living together in harmony,
nation existing peaceably alongside nation,
people set free to be themselves –
valued,
loved,
respected,
not for what we can get out of them,
but simply for what they are.
Is that so daft?
Well, yes, it probably is,
for nine times out of ten,
ninety-nine times out of a hundred,
for most of us, when the pressure's on,
it's number one who comes first,
a question of 'I'm all right and never mind the rest'.
We'd like it to be different, obviously,
but even when we're not simply paying lip-service to high ideals,
we can't finally change ourselves, try as we might.
Yet give me one thing –
it's an incredible idea, isn't it,
this world of peace and justice? –
a beautiful picture,
worth striving for, I'd say,
even worth dying for.
And who knows, one day,
just maybe,
somebody might actually come along
with the faith and courage not just to dream about it,
but to bring it about;
not simply to share the vision,
but to live in such a way that it becomes real –
God's kingdom, here on earth.

Prayer

Gracious God,
    I look at the world sometimes,
    and I despair.
I see its greed, corruption, hatred and violence,
    and I can't help asking,
    'How will it ever change?'
    I want to believe,
    and occasionally my hopes are rekindled
    by moves towards peace,
    yet it is hard to keep faith
    when, time after time, such initiatives come to nothing.
Gracious God,
    help me to recognise that my way of looking at the world
    is not the same as your way,
    and that where I see no prospect of change
    you are able to transform situations beyond recognition.
Teach me never to lose sight of all that you are able to do
    and all that you are already doing.
Inspire me, therefore, to pray for, and in my own small way
    work towards, peace and reconciliation.
Through Jesus Christ my Lord.
Amen.

4
Where did it all start?
John, the Apostle

There is something unusual about the Gospel of John. Unlike Matthew and Luke, John does not start with Mary or Joseph, nor does he refer to Bethlehem, a stable or a manger; in fact, there is no mention of a Christmas story at all. Unlike Mark, he does not start with the ministry of Jesus, though he soon moves on to this. Instead he takes us back to the dawn of time and the events of creation, as he reminds us once more of God's sovereign will, operative at the beginning of it all. Despite everything that would frustrate him and deny his love, he tells us, God's gracious purpose has always been at work expressed through his living Word, later embodied in the Word made flesh. For John, the coming of Christ was not God's attempt to make up for a ghastly mistake; it was the natural expression of a love constantly at work, revealed in history, declared through prophets, and finally lived out in flesh and blood. John's testimony calls us to reflect on all God has yet to do in the light of everything he has already done.

Reading: John 1:1-5, 10-14

In the beginning was the Word, and the Word was with God, and the Word was God. He was in the beginning with God. All things came into being through him, and nothing could exist without him. What has come into being in him is life, and that life is the light of all people. The light shines in the darkness, and the darkness has not overcome it. He was in the world, and the world came into being through him; but the world did not know him. He came into what was his own, and his own people did not accept him. To all, though, who did receive him and believed in his name, he gave the right to become children of God; children born not of blood or any union of the flesh, nor of any human desire, but of God. The Word became flesh and lived among us, and we have seen his glory, the glory as of a father's only son, full of grace and truth.

Meditation

'Where did it all start?' they ask me.
'Tell us the story again.'
And I know just what they want to hear –
    about the inn and the stable,
    the baby lying in a manger,
    shepherds out in the fields by night,
    and wise men travelling from afar.
I know why they ask, of course I do,
    for which of us hasn't thrilled to those marvellous events,
    that astonishing day when the Word became flesh,
    dwelling here on earth amongst us?
Yet wonderful though that all is, it's not where it started,
    and if we stop there, then we see only a fraction of the picture,
    the merest glimpse of everything God has done for us in Christ.
We have to go right back to see more –
    before Bethlehem,
    before the prophets
    before the Law,
    before time itself, would you believe? –
    for that's where it started:
    literally 'In the beginning'.
Yes, even there the saving purpose of God was at work,
    his creating, redeeming Word
    bringing light and love into the world,

shaping not just the heavens and the earth but the lives of all,
every man, woman and child.
That's the mind-boggling wonder of it –
the fact not just that God made us,
but that through Christ he was determined from the outset
to share our lives,
to take on our flesh,
to identify himself totally with the joys and sorrows,
the beauty and the ugliness, of humankind.
It defies belief, doesn't it?
Yet it's true –
God wanted us to know him not as his creatures
but as his children,
not as puppets forced to dance to his tune
but as people responding freely to his love,
and to do that he patiently and painstakingly prepared the way,
revealing year after year a little more of his purpose,
a glimpse more of his kingdom,
until at last,
in the fullness of time,
the Word became flesh and lived among us full of grace and truth.
It wasn't an afterthought, the incarnation,
a last-ditch attempt to make the best of a bad job –
it was planned from the dawn of time.
So next time you hear the story of the stable and the manger,
of the shepherds gazing in wonder
and the magi kneeling in homage,
stop for a moment and reflect
on everything that made it all possible,
the eternal purpose that so carefully prepared the way of Christ,
and then rejoice that this same purpose
embraces not simply others,
but includes you!

Prayer

Gracious God,
    despite my repeated disobedience,
    your love continues undiminished,
    reaching out to me every moment of every day.
Despite the rejection of the world,
    still you go on seeking to draw people closer to you,
    longing to establish a living relationship with each and every one.
So it is now and so it has always been,
    from the beginning of time your nature always to have mercy.
Help me to appreciate the enormity of your faithfulness,
    and to use this season of Advent
    to open my heart more fully to your grace.
Through Jesus Christ my Lord.
Amen.

5
How did we feel about him?
Zechariah

What is the job of witnesses in a court case? Is it to give details about themselves and their life? To a point, yes, but only in so far as such details relate, directly or indirectly, to the defendant. Ultimately, their task is to throw light on someone else rather than themselves. Here is the key to understanding the life of John the Baptist, the one who came as 'a voice in the wilderness' to prepare the way of Christ. Despite the considerable following that built up around him, his distinctive lifestyle and powerful preaching were not designed to draw attention to himself but to point towards Christ and so prepare the way of his coming. As the gospel of John puts it: 'He personally was not the light, but he came to bear witness to the light' (John 1:8). Undoubtedly, the role of John the Baptist was special but that does not mean he has nothing to teach us. On the contrary, we need to echo his example, for Jesus calls us in turn to bear witness to him. Do we honestly do that? Do we seek his glory rather than our own? How far, if at all, do we help prepare the way for Christ's coming into the hearts and minds of people today?

Reading: Luke 1:16-17, 76-79

He will turn many of the people of Israel to the Lord their God, and he will go out in the spirit and power of Elijah to turn the hearts of parents to their children, and the disobedient to the wisdom of the righteous – to prepare people so that they are ready for the Lord. You, child, will be called the prophet of the Most High; for you will go before the Lord to prepare his ways, to give knowledge of salvation to his people by the forgiveness of their sins. By the tender mercy of our God, the dawn from on high will break upon us, to give light to those who sit in darkness and in the shadow of death, to guide our feet into the way of peace.

Meditation

How did we feel about him?
Well, you don't really need to ask, do you?
We were more proud than words can say.
To think that our lad, John, should be the one
    spoken of by the prophet,
      chosen to proclaim the coming of the Messiah,
    to announce the dawn of his kingdom.
What an honour!
What a privilege!
The very thought of it still takes our breath away!
To tell the truth, we've had to be careful sometimes
    not to get carried away,
    not to put our son on a pedestal
    as though *he* were one God had promised;
    heaven knows he's special enough to us.
Yet if ever we fell into that trap, he soon put us right,
    reminding us, in no uncertain terms, just what his role is
    in the great scheme of things.
It's funny how he knows,
    for we've never spelt it out to him,
    never had any need to –
    he seems to have understood from the very beginning
    what God expects from him.
You only had to see him as a boy to recognise that,
    the way he acted towards Jesus, especially –

it was as though he had a special responsibility towards him,
   and I swear sometimes there was a hint of admiration in his eyes,
   even awe as they played together!
If anything it's become more apparent as the years have passed –
   a special bond developing between them,
   but there's always been an element of distance too,
   a sense, on John's part anyway,
   of getting this close and no further,
   as though there's a gulf in status between them
   which he would never presume to cross.
Not everyone could do that, could they? –
   accept a supporting role rather than a position centre-stage –
   but there's never been a hint of resentment,
   still less any desire to thrust himself forward.
A voice in the wilderness, that's how he describes himself,
   sent to prepare the way of the Lord,
   to make straight his path in readiness for his kingdom –
   and he's shown since exactly what that means.
Not that he's the only one who longs for that day,
   we've all prayed for it for as long as I can remember.
The difference is that John doesn't simply talk about it,
   he's helping to make it happen:
   his actions as well as his words,
   his whole life, in fact,
   a daily witness to the change God requires of us –
   a foretaste, if you like, of that transformation he holds in store.
You think you're ready for his coming,
   ready to welcome the Messiah?
Well maybe you are,
   but before you get too complacent, just ask yourself this:
   What are you doing to bring his kingdom closer? –
   for until you can answer that, take it from me,
   you're nowhere near ready at all.

Prayer

Lord Jesus Christ,
    help me, like John the Baptist,
    to point not to myself but to you.
Help me to speak faithfully of your love
    and to live in a way that gives credence to my words.
By your grace, may I prepare your way in turn,
    testifying to everything you have done in my life,
    and so may the hearts of many be made ready
    to receive you today.
In your name, I ask it.
Amen.

6
'You've got it wrong!' I told him
Mary

Surely, God can't use me? How often have we echoed the response of Mary when God has asked something of us? He can use others maybe, but not me – I don't possess the necessary gifts or qualities; I lack sufficient faith, trust and commitment. The response is all the more vociferous when what God is asking involves sacrifice on our part. Yet, if Mary's initial response is perfectly understandable, how then do we account for her compliance with God's wishes just a few moments afterwards, her willingness to swallow her reservations and accept his will? The answer is simple – she measured what was being asked of her not against her own resources but against God's. She knew her weaknesses, but she also understood God's strength. She was aware of her limitations, but equally she recognised God's sovereignty, his ability to do whatever he wills. So it was that, instead of procrastinating, she offered acceptance – no doubt still confused, still unsure of herself, still wondering quite how and why she had been chosen, but ready to let God use her as he saw fit.

Advent calls for a similar response from us today, if the one at its centre is to become a part of our lives. We can warm to accounts of the birth of Jesus, we can celebrate his life and ministry, we can give intellectual assent to the lordship of Christ, and we may be fascinated, intrigued, even moved by it all, but God wants more than that. He wants us to be *changed*: our lives turned around, our experience revolutionised, our very self re-created through his grace. He wants us to become part of his people and to use us in the work of his kingdom. 'Who, me?' we may say; 'Surely not!' – and that, of course, brings us back to where we started: to the quiet trusting response of Mary to God's call. It is a response that resounds across the centuries, speaking loud and clear today: 'Yes, you!'

Reading: Luke 1:26-38

Now in the sixth month the angel Gabriel was sent by God to a town in Galilee called Nazareth, to a virgin engaged to a man named Joseph, a member of the house of David. The virgin's name was Mary. Approaching her, he said, 'Greetings, you who have been highly favoured. The Lord is with you.' She was bewildered by his words, and contemplated what such a greeting might mean. The angel said to her, 'Don't be frightened, Mary, for you have found favour with God, for you will conceive in your womb and bear a son, and you will give him the name "Jesus". He will be great, and will be called the Son of the Most High, and the Lord God will give him the throne of his ancestor David. He will reign over the house of Jacob for ever, and his kingdom will never end.' Mary said to the angel, 'How can this be, since I am a virgin?' The angel answered, 'The Holy Spirit will come upon you, and the power of the Most High will rest over you, so that the child you will bear will be called the Son of God. Even your relative Elizabeth, in her old age, has conceived a son; she who was said to be barren now in her sixth month, for with God nothing is impossible.' Mary responded, 'I am the Lord's servant. Let it be to me just as you say.'

Meditation

'You've got it wrong!' I told him.
'You can't mean me,
    no way!
Someone else perhaps,
    more worthy,
    more important,
    but not me!'
Honestly, what did I have to commend me?
No connections or special qualities,
    nothing –

just an ordinary girl from Nazareth –
so what could God see in me?
But it was academic anyway, for I wasn't even married yet,
and there was no way I'd sleep with Joseph until I was.
So I came straight out with it:
'Sorry, but you're wrong!'
Only he wouldn't take no for an answer.
Just stood there smiling,
unruffled;
and before I knew it he was off again –
the message even more fantastic than before –
God's power overshadowing me,
a child born of the Holy Spirit,
the Son of God!
It was way over the top,
and I should have turned him out there and then,
but I was flummoxed,
too amazed to reply.
Even when I found my tongue it wasn't much use to me –
can you believe it, my mind brimming over with questions
and what did I say? –
'Here am I, the servant of the Lord,
let it be to me according to your word.'
Oh, it sounded good, granted –
the epitome of humility –
but if you only knew what I was thinking,
you'd have a different picture then.
So what got into me, you ask?
How could I be so meek and accepting?
Well, what choice did I have, let's be honest,
for as the angel said, 'With God, nothing will be impossible.'
How could I argue with that?
There was no way out, was there?
But it's one thing to accept that in principle,
another when it turns your life upside down.
Do I believe it?

31

Well, I didn't at the time,
   but I do now,
   for I've just discovered I'm pregnant,
   and I say this perfectly reverently, God knows how!
It's astonishing and terrifying,
   exciting yet mystifying,
   my mind in turmoil, not quite sure what to think any more.
But one thing is plain now,
   beyond all question –
   with him quite clearly nothing *is* impossible!

Prayer

Gracious God,
   you may not ask of me what you asked of Mary,
   but none the less you call me to service,
   and sometimes that involves things I feel to be beyond me.
Teach me, at such times,
   never to underestimate your sovereign power.
Grant me humility to hear your voice
   and faith to respond.
Like Mary, may I be ready when you call to answer:
   'Here am I, the servant of the Lord;
   let it be to me according to your word.'
Through Jesus Christ my Lord.
Amen.

7
It was the strangest of dreams
Joseph

If there's one thing harder than accepting God can use *you*, then its accepting he can use someone else, especially when that 'someone' is close to you. We think we know all about them, and, almost certainly, their faults and weaknesses are clearer to us than to most people. Any suggestion that God has singled them out for a special purpose is often met with more than a raised eyebrow. When those faults are writ large, then it's all the harder to believe. What must it have looked like, then, to Joseph when Mary broke the news that she was pregnant, only to tell him in the next breath that the child she carried was not the result of some illicit liaison but was the Son of God? How would you have responded in his shoes? A little scepticism was perfectly understandable. Yet Joseph, like Mary, was willing to let God overturn his preconceptions, ready to accept that God could use this girl he thought he knew so well in the most remarkable of ways.

The circumstances in this case were, admittedly, remarkable, but the principle holds none the less for us all. We need to be open to God working through those we might least expect; and, above all, through those we are so close to that we mistakenly imagine we know everything there is to know about them. It may be that it is time to think again!

Reading: Matthew 1:18-25

This is what happened concerning the birth of Jesus Christ. While his mother, Mary, was engaged to Joseph, but before they lived together, she became pregnant, through the Holy Spirit. Being a good man unwilling to expose her to public disgrace, Joseph planned to quietly end the engagement. However, just when he had made this decision, an angel of the Lord appeared to him in a dream and said, 'Joseph, son of David, do not be afraid to take Mary as your wife, for the child conceived within her is from the Holy Spirit. She will bear a son, and you are to call him Jesus, for he will save his people from their sins.' All this took place to fulfil what the Lord had spoken through the prophet: 'Look, the virgin will conceive and bear a son, and they will call him Emmanuel', which means, 'God is with us'. After waking from his sleep, Joseph did as the angel of the Lord had instructed, taking Mary as his wife, but he had no sexual relations with her until she gave birth to a son; and he named him Jesus.

Meditation

It was the strangest of dreams,
   ludicrous really,
    yet I just can't get it out of my mind.
You see, I dreamt God was speaking to me.
No, not face to face, I don't mean that,
   but through this angel, claiming to be his special messenger.
And do you know what he told me?
Take Mary to be your wife, that's what.
Just when I'd decided to put her quietly aside,
   hush up the scandal as best I could,
   this character telling me to think again.
And why?
Because apparently it was nothing to do with her,
   the baby she's carrying not the result of some fleeting passion,
   but conceived of the Holy Spirit,
   ordained by God himself.
Well, I've heard a few excuses in my time
   but that one really takes the biscuit!
I mean, who did the fellow think I was – some fool born yesterday?

It was laughable,
    and I'd usually have dismissed it without a second thought.
Yet I didn't –
    not then,
    not now.
A dream it may have been,
    but it's lived with me,
    as vivid today as when I first dreamt it.
I can't say why exactly –
    it was a mixture of things, I suppose.
There was Mary for a start,
    the way she looked at me as she broke the news –
    so trusting,
    so innocent,
    almost as though she too had met with God
    and was confident I would understand.
Then there was Elizabeth and Zechariah –
    heaven knows what got into them,
    but they were simply delighted,
    no hint of suspicion, let alone scandal, so far as they saw it –
    I suppose that boy of theirs, after so many disappointments,
    was enough to turn anyone's mind.
But what really swung it was this feeling deep within
    that somehow God had touched me;
    that, like it or not, life was changed for ever.
I was right in that, wasn't I?
    for we're on the road to Bethlehem as I speak,
    my wife heavy with child,
    wincing with pain,
    praying it's not much further.
Did I do right, standing by her?
I still have my doubts, even now,
    still find it hard to meet her eye,
    for it takes some getting used to, a child you had no part in –
    but, despite the questions, I've done my best for her,
    taking her for my wife, just as I was told.

Now it's God's turn, isn't it? –
    over to him for the Saviour to be born,
    God with us!
Was it a dream, a figment of my imagination?
We'll soon see, won't we?

Prayer

Gracious God,
    you act in ways I do not expect,
    you speak in ways I do not always understand,
    you come at times and in places I least imagine,
    and all too easily I fail to recognise your presence.
Teach me to be awake to your prompting,
    however unlikely it may seem,
    and help me to respond whenever you call,
    even though I have no idea where it all might lead.
Equip me to walk in faith.
Through Jesus Christ my Lord.
Amen.

8

I felt sorry for that couple
The innkeeper

Anyone who has ever commuted by train to London will know all about the problems of making room. Carriages are already full to overflowing as the train pulls into another station heaving with yet more people. Somehow, yet more squeeze in, wedged together nose to tail like sardines. Again, you may have travelled to the coast on a bank holiday weekend or in the height of summer, looking for a hotel or B&B to stay in, only in every window to see the same depressing sign: 'No Vacancies'. The situation must have been a little like that in Bethlehem on the night of Jesus' birth. People of the house and line of David had come from across Judea to be enrolled in the Roman census, cramming into every home, guest house and inn. We can scarcely imagine what Mary and Joseph must have gone through as they searched desperately for somewhere to stay overnight, Mary's labour pains getting stronger by the minute. That experience, of course, was a symbol of things to come, Jesus finding no room in the hearts of many throughout his ministry and continuing to find no room in the hearts of many today.

We may imagine that *we* are different; that we have opened the door of our lives and welcomed him in; but let's not be complacent about it. The truth is that most of us only half open the door, at best. We allow Jesus access to certain areas of our life but keep other areas ring-fenced. We allow him in at certain times but not at others. We make room when it suits us, but at other times give him our divided attention if any at all. It is easy to fool ourselves that such a response will do, when, in reality, Jesus is knocking at the door, still asking to come in. Are we prepared to keep him on the fringe of our life, or are we ready to give him the place he deserves?

Reading: Luke 2:1-7

It happened at that time that Caesar Augustus issued a decree that a census should be taken of the entire world. This was the first such census and occurred while Quirinius was governor of Syria. All, therefore, went to be registered, each to their appropriate town. Joseph, being of the house and family of David, went from the Galilean town of Nazareth to Judea, to the city of David called Bethlehem, to be registered with his fiancée Mary, who was expecting a child. While they were there, she went into labour and gave birth to her firstborn son. She swaddled him in strips of cloth, and laid him in a manger, because there was no room for them in the inn.

Meditation

I felt sorry for that couple, I really did.
They were at their wits end, the pair of them,
    just about all in.
But it was the woman who concerned me most;
    fit to drop she was,
    and hardly a surprise given her condition –
    not that I'm an expert in these matters,
    but I felt sure her pains had already started;
    and so it was to prove, poor lass.
As for him, he was beside himself,
    frantic with worry,
    almost abusive in his frustration;
    and I can't say I blamed him –
    I'd have been the same in the circumstances.
Yet what could I do?
There wasn't a room to spare – that was the fact of the matter.
We were packed already,
    bulging at the seams,
    and I could hardly turf someone else out just to fit them in,
        could I?

I mean, be reasonable, that would have caused a right-old to-do,
    no use to anybody.
So I offered them the stable, if they could make use of it.
Not much of a prospect I agree,
    especially on such a night as that turned out,
    but it was a roof over their heads,
    a shelter from the worst of the wind if nothing else.
All right, so I still feel bad about it,
wish now I'd taken my wife's advice
    and given up our room for them,
    but to be honest we were both whacked,
    what with all the extra custom to see to.
We had an inn to run, remember, and we were rushed off our feet,
    longing only for a good night's sleep ourselves.
So we gave them the stable and that's the end of it –
    no point brooding over what might have been.
And to be fair, they were grateful,
    glad of anywhere to put their heads down.
But when I heard the baby crying, that's when it got to me –
    out there in those conditions!
I felt ashamed,
    disgusted with myself.
So we hurried out, the wife and I,
    anxious to help,
    not sure what we might find, though fearing the worst.
But what a suprise!
There was no panic,
    no sign of confusion.
Quite the contrary –
    they seemed so peaceful,
    so full of joy,
    utterly content.
And the way they looked at that child –
    I mean, I've heard of worshipping your kids
    but this was something else –

they were over the moon,
    absolutely ecstatic!
And that wasn't the half of it,
    for suddenly there in the shadows I spotted a bunch of shepherds –
    God knows where they came from.
I thought for a moment they were up to no good,
    but they weren't –
    they just stood there gawping into the manger,
    wide-eyed with wonder,
    almost as though they'd never seen a baby before!
And then they walked away,
    joy in their faces,
    delight in their steps.
It's all quiet now, the inn and the stable,
    as if that night had never happened.
And, as far as I know, both mother and child are well.
You could say that's down to me in part,
    for at least I did something to help if no one else did.
Yet I can't help feeling I should have done more,
    that I let everyone down somehow –
    that it wasn't finally them left out in the cold,
    it was me.

Prayer

Lord Jesus Christ,
    I remember today how you came to our world
    and found no welcome;
    how, from the very beginning, you were shut out,
    no room for you even in the inn.
Forgive me that I too am guilty sometimes of shutting you out,
    failing to make room for you not only at Christmas
    but also in so many areas of my life.

Despite my words of faith and commitment,
    I fail to make time for you as I should
    and turn my back on you
    when I would rather not face your challenge.
Forgive me, and help me to make room for you,
    not just this Christmas but always.
Teach me to give you not just a token place in my heart,
    but to put you at the very centre of my life.
Come now, and make your home within me,
    by your grace.
Amen.

9
He looked so tiny lying there
Mary

I had to look twice when I first saw it. A week of autumn gales had battered virtually everything in the garden, but there, on a bedraggled-looking rose bush, was a single perfect bloom, untouched by the storms. How anything so delicate and vulnerable could have survived unscathed was beyond me, but somehow it had done just that, withstanding everything that the world could throw against it. In a sense, we see something similar, though yet more remarkable, in the birth of Jesus. Here, we are told, was the creator of the universe, the Lord of heaven and earth, lying in a manger. Here was the one before and beyond time, as frail and vulnerable as a newborn baby. Here was God made flesh! That is what the Incarnation is all about: God taking on our humanity, making himself vulnerable to the point of death, staking his saving purpose on flesh and blood like you and me. Have you considered what that means? Here is a classic case of God's strength in weakness, using the seemingly fragile and insignificant to fulfil his purpose. That truth holds for each of us today. We may feel incapable of achieving anything in God's service, or of making any impact on those around us. We may feel battered by the storms of life, unsure of our ability to get through. The coming of Christ, born in a stable, reminds us that God is able to use what the world counts weak in ways beyond our imagining.

Reading: Luke 2:6-7a

While they were there, she went into labour and gave birth to her firstborn son. She swaddled him in strips of cloth, and laid him in a manger.

Meditation

He looked so tiny lying there,
    so vulnerable –
    like a little china doll,
    like thistledown swaying in the breeze –
    and I wanted simply to hold him in my arms
    and protect him from the world outside.
Could this be God's son, I asked,
    the one destined to be great,
    the Prince of Peace,
    a ruler over Israel?
Surely not!
It had been hard enough to believe at the start,
    when the angel first broke the news –
    to think that I, Mary, had been chosen above all others,
    singled out to bear in my womb the Messiah –
    but now, as I gazed down into the manger,
    and saw that sweet innocent face wrinkled up in sleep,
    and those eyes so tightly shut,
    it seemed doubly impossible,
    out of the question,
    a foolish fancy of my fevered imagination.
Be sensible, I told myself,
    there's no way God could take such a gamble,
    no possibility, if the fate of the world truly hung in the balance,
    that he would stake it all on a helpless child,
    least of all born where we ended up – a stable of all places!
And, as if to prove the point, that very moment Jesus awoke,
    tears filling his eyes,
    a scream of protest on his lips,
    and I realised he was hungry,
    well past his usual feed.
It dawned on me then, the staggering implications –
    he needed me, this child,
    not just for food, or warmth, or protection,

but for everything,
    his very future in my hands.
Would God allow that?
Could he ever need *us* as much as *we* need him?
No, there had to be some mistake –
    it just couldn't be, could it?
Could it?

Prayer

Gracious God,
    I marvel that you were ready to share my humanity,
    entering this world as a frail and defenceless child.
I praise you for your willingness to stake everything
    to fulfil your saving purpose,
    becoming one with *us*,
    so that we might become one with *you*.
In weakness, you showed strength,
    and in what the world counted as nothing, you gave everything.
Teach me what that means,
    and help me to remember
    that you are able to work today in my life,
    even when I feel I have nothing to offer.
Take me then, and work through me, by your grace.
Through Jesus Christ my Lord.
Amen.

10
It was just an ordinary day
Shepherds

'There were shepherds living in the fields by night, keeping watch over their flocks by night.' Those are words that somehow automatically evoke an idyllic pastoral scene; a picture of shepherds out in the gathering dusk, faithfully tending to their flock – loyal, dependable, dedicated. No doubt they were all of these, but that's not the message Luke wants us to take away from these verses. In the Judea of Luke's day, shepherding was a lonely and demanding business that involved long antisocial hours and consequently meant that shepherds were often unable to attend temple worship or share in the life of their community. In other words, they were seen as ordinary, at best, and, more likely as not, as villains to be treated with suspicion.

Yet it was these, says Luke, whom God chose to be the first to hear the good news; not the religious elite, nor the rich, the respectable and the revered, but those counted as nothing and less than nothing. It was a pattern that Jesus was to continue throughout his ministry, calling fishermen, a tax-collector and a zealot as his disciples, and mixing with 'tax collectors and sinners', to the shock of the scribes and Pharisees. Here is a reminder of the God who has time for anyone, whoever that person may be; who has time for everyone, whatever they may have done. Here is the God who has time for you!

Reading: Luke 2:8-16

There were shepherds in that area, living in the fields and keeping watch over their flock during the night. Suddenly, an angel of the Lord appeared to them, and the glory of the Lord shone around them, and they were overcome with terror. However, the angel said to them, 'Don't be frightened, for see – I am bringing you good news of great joy that is for all people: today a Saviour has been born to you in the city of David, who is the Christ, the Lord. Let this be a sign to you: you will find a child swaddled in strips of cloth and lying in a manger.' All at once, there was with the angel rank on rank of other heavenly beings, praising God and saying, 'Glory to God in the highest heaven, and peace on earth among all on whom his favour rests!'

When the angels had departed and returned to heaven, the shepherds said to each other, 'Let us go, then, to Bethlehem and see this event that has taken place, which the Lord has made known to us.' So they came with haste, and found Mary and Joseph, and the baby lying in a manger.

Meditation

It was just an ordinary day, that's what I can't get over;
    nothing special about it,
    nothing different,
    just another ordinary day.
And we were all just ordinary people,
    that's what made it even more puzzling;
    not important,
    not influential,
    just plain ordinary shepherds out working in the fields.
Yet we apparently were the first,
    singled out for special favour!
The first to know,
    the first to see,
    the first to celebrate,
    the first to tell!
I'm still not sure what happened –
    one moment night drawing in,
    and the next bright as day;

one moment laughing and joking together,
and the next rooted to the spot in amazement;
one moment looking forward to getting home,
and the next hurrying down to Bethlehem.
There just aren't words to express what we felt,
but we knew we had to respond,
had to go and see for ourselves.
Not that we expected to find anything, mind you,
not if we were honest.
Well, you don't, do you?
I mean, it's not every day the Messiah arrives, is it?
And we'd always imagined when he finally did,
it would be in a blaze of glory,
to a fanfare of trumpets,
with the maximum of publicity.
Yet do you know what?
When we got there,
it was to find everything just as we had been told;
wonderfully special,
yet surprisingly ordinary.
Not Jerusalem but Bethlehem,
not a palace but a stable,
not a prince enthroned in splendour but a baby lying in a manger.
We still find it hard to believe even now,
to think God chose to come through that tiny vulnerable child.
But as the years have passed
and we've seen not just his birth but his life,
and not just his life but his death,
and not just his death but his empty tomb,
his graveclothes, his joyful followers,
we've slowly come to realise it really was true.
God had chosen to come to us,
and more than that, to you –
to ordinary, everyday people,
in the most ordinary, everyday of ways.
How extraordinary!

Prayer

Lord Jesus Christ,
    I am reminded today
    that it wasn't the important in the eyes of the world
    who first heard the good news,
    nor the religious elite,
    but shepherds – ordinary, everyday people like me.
Teach me, through their story,
    that however insignificant I may feel,
    you value me for what I am;
    and teach me in turn to recognise the value of all,
    for your name's sake.
Amen.

11
Have you heard the news?
Resident of Bethlehem

If I were to say to you the words 'made for sharing', what word or words would you automatically insert before them to make what, at one time at least, was a well-known catchphrase? The chances are that you would think of that old advertisement 'Quality Street, made for sharing'. I, though, have something very different in mind: the word 'Christmas'. You will see some logic in that straightaway, for Christmas is traditionally a time for sharing cards, presents and good wishes. It is a time also when families come together and share in a way that may not be possible during the rest of the year. For Christians, it is also a time for sharing in worship: nativity, candlelight and carol services. Yet, special and important though all those things are, I have one more thing in mind; something we see in the example of the shepherds. 'When they had seen him, they spread the word' (Luke 2:17). Think about that, for a moment, and then ask how far it is reflected in your life. Having seen Jesus, the shepherds' instinctive response was to want to share it; to tell others the good news; to make sure that others heard about what God had done. This wasn't something to keep to themselves, nor an event staged solely for their own benefit. In the words of the angel, it was 'news of great joy for all people'. I've no doubt we will share much this Christmas, and hopefully what we give will bring those nearest and dearest to us great joy, but will we share the greatest gift of all? Will we communicate what we have experienced, or will we act as though God's gift is for us and no one else? 'Christmas, made for sharing' – is that how you see it?

Reading: Luke 2:16-20

They came with haste, and found Mary and Joseph, and the baby lying in a manger. Having seen it, they shared everything they had been told concerning the child, and all those who heard them marvelled at what the shepherds said to them. Mary, though, stored these things up in her heart, pondering what they might mean. The shepherds returned, glorifying and praising God for everything they had heard and seen, just as they had been told.

Meditation

Have you heard the news?
They're saying the Messiah's been born,
   right here in Bethlehem!
Honestly, that's what I was told,
   the Christ,
   God's promised deliverer,
   come at last to set us free.
Do I believe it?
Well, I'm not sure.
It's hard to credit, I admit,
   but this friend I spoke to seemed pretty certain.
Heard it from a shepherd apparently,
   some chap who claimed to have seen the child for himself,
   and by all accounts he was delirious with excitement,
   absolutely full of it.
He may have been mistaken, of course,
   or simply spinning some old yarn –
   you never can be sure, can you?
And, believe me, I don't go round believing everything I hear.
But this friend of mine,
   the one who heard it from the shepherd,
   he was full of it too.

You would have thought he'd been there,
   in the stable,
   beside the manger,
   the way he spoke.
He was utterly convinced, there's no question about that,
   and as I listened to him chattering on,
     I felt the urge welling up inside me, just as he had done,
     to tell someone else,
     to share the good news with those around me.
If he was right, then this wasn't something to keep to myself,
   nor for the privileged few,
   but a message for everybody;
   one they all needed to hear.
But before I say anything more,
   risk making a complete fool of myself,
   there's something I have to do,
   something my friend should have done
   and which the shepherds presumably did,
   and that is go and see for myself.
Call me a cynic of you like but I believe it's important,
   no, more than that, vital,
   for if you're going to accept something,
   let alone expect others to do the same,
   you have to be sure of your ground,
   as certain as you can be that it's not just all some grand delusion.
So I'm going now, off to find out the truth for myself,
   off to see this child, if he really exists, with my own eyes.
And if I find everything just as I've been told,
   the baby lying there in a manger, wrapped in strips of cloth,
   then I shall go and tell others what I have seen,
   for – let's be honest – what else would there be to do?
What else could anybody do in my place?

Prayer

Living God,
    I remember today
    how shepherds responded to the message of the angels –
    how they hurried to Bethlehem
    and found the baby lying in a manger,
    and how afterwards they went on their way,
    sharing what they had seen and heard.
Teach me to share my experience of Christ in turn.
Help me to understand that your coming through him
    is good news for everyone,
    and that you want me to help make that known.
So, help me to live each day with joy in my heart
    and wonder in my eyes,
    as I share the love that you have shown
    and make known the great things that you have done in Christ.
In his name, I ask it.
Amen.

12
There was something about that couple
Priest

How would you react if you had just heard some good news? If you'd just won the football pools or National Lottery, or just met the partner of your dreams, or if you'd won promotion at work or won the holiday of a lifetime, would you keep it quiet? Would you carry on as if nothing had happened? Would you manage to control every flicker of emotion that might betray what had happened? I doubt it.

So how did Mary and Joseph react to the news that their child was to be the Son of God, the promised deliverer and long-awaited Messiah? More important, how did they respond when the great day finally came and Jesus was born? The fact is that we don't know, but that very fact seems to indicate that neither Mary nor Joseph went around telling everyone that the Messiah had been born to them. Yet, could they have kept the awe and the wonder they must surely have felt entirely hidden? It seems unlikely, to say the least. Something must have shown in their eyes, their voices and their demeanour. The following meditation poses that question from the perspective of the priest who welcomed Mary and Joseph at the temple as they came, in accordance with Jewish law, to present their eight-day-old child to the Lord. What was he able to read from their manner? We can only guess, but I'd be surprised if nothing of their joy at what God had done for them shone through, and that brings me back to our first question: How do we react to good news? It's not just an academic question, because, of course, we *have heard* good news – the gospel of Jesus Christ. Do we keep it to ourselves? Is it simply a matter of private celebration? According to Jesus, even if we were to say nothing, our lives should shine like a light in the world in such a way that people cannot help but notice and give glory to God. No, that doesn't mean that people will take one look at us and automatically know that we are Christians, but there should be a sense of joy and wonder in our lives that is contagious; an unmistakable air of celebration that leaves people asking the question: What is it they've got that I haven't? – and that consequently inspires them to find out for themselves.

Reading: Luke 2:21-24, 39-40

When eight days had passed, the time came to circumcise the child; and they called him Jesus, the name the angel had given even before conception. When the time came for him to be purified according to the law of Moses, they brought him to Jerusalem to present him to the Lord (as it is written in the law of the Lord, 'Every firstborn male shall be designated as holy to the Lord'), and they offered a sacrifice as prescribed in the law of the Lord, 'a pair of turtledoves or two young pigeons'. When they had done everything the law of the Lord required, they returned to their hometown of Nazareth in Galilee. The child grew in strength and wisdom; and God's favour rested on him.

Meditation

There was something about that couple,
    something that caught my attention the moment I saw them.
Happiness, I suppose it was,
    the joy of sharing a newborn baby.
Only it was more than that,
    for I've seen a multitude of parents over the years,
    each coming bubbling with excitement,
    skipping with delight,
    and yet none had that look of wide-eyed wonder which these
        had.

It was as though they thought their child different from any other,
    a unique gift from God to be handled with infinite care,
    treasured beyond all price.
Oh, I know every parent feels their baby's special –
    in their eyes the most beautiful thing ever born –
    yet with these two it was more than that.
It was almost as if they were in awe of the child,
    elated yet terrified at the responsibility of parenthood.
You think I'm exaggerating,
    reading too much into an innocent moment?
Well, possibly.
She was very young, after all,
    and this was their first child –
    everything new,
    unknown,
    unexplored.
Yet I still say I've never seen a look quite like they had.
Probably it will always remain a mystery,
    for though, no doubt, they'll come back
    for the occasional festival or ceremony,
    I'm not sure I'll recognise them when they do.
Yet perhaps I may find the answer despite that,
    for when his mother handed me the child,
    and announced his name – Jesus –
    she did so as if it should mean something to me,
    as if I would understand straightaway
    why the child was so important,
    as if he was a gift not just to *them*,
    but to *me*,
    to *you*,
    and to *everyone*.

Prayer

Gracious God,
  I remember today the joy you brought through Jesus
  to those whose lives were touched by his birth –
  Mary, Joseph, shepherds, magi, Simeon and Anna –
  their lives overflowing with praise and thanksgiving.
Forgive me that the joy I have felt in turn
  can sometimes be lost as the years go by,
  dulled by familiarity or swamped by the cares of daily life.
Speak the good news to me again
  and enter my heart afresh,
  so that I may know once more
  the gladness that only Christ can bring.
In his name, I ask it.
Amen.

13
We knew it would be worth it
Magi

We had been travelling for hours and yet still, it seemed, we were no nearer our destination. Just why was a mystery, for we had carefully followed the map, or at least we thought we had, but somehow or somewhere we must have taken a wrong turning. Was it worth continuing? We'd both begun to wonder. Yet the guidebook had stressed that this was a sight not to be missed, a vista unparalleled in that part of the country, so we decided on one last attempt. A good thing too, for this time we made it, and it proved more than worth all the effort. 'Seek,' said Jesus, 'and you will find', and when he said 'seek', he meant it. He didn't have in mind casually looking for something and then giving up, but was speaking rather of a willingness to search and keep on searching for as long as it takes.

We see a vivid example of that in the journey of the wise men and their quest for the newborn king. It would have been so easy for them to abandon their search, not least when they arrived in Bethlehem to find that no one had any idea what they were talking about. Could there have been some mistake? Had their journey been a waste of time? Yet they kept on searching and trusting until, finally, they came to the place where the child lay. We, too, need to seek today, and our search does not end when we enter into a personal relationship with Christ. On the contrary, we realise then how far we have yet to grow and how much more there is yet to understand, faith not a destination but a journey. Are we ready to keep on searching?

Reading: Matthew 2:1-12

After Jesus had been born in Bethlehem of Judea, during the reign of King Herod, wise men arrived in Jerusalem from the East, asking, 'Where is the one born the king of the Jews? For we saw his star in the East, and so have come to pay him homage.' On hearing this, King Herod was alarmed, and all Jerusalem with him; and, having assembled all the chief priests and scribes of the people, he asked them where the Messiah was to be born. They told him, 'In Bethlehem of Judea; for so it has been written by the prophet: "And you, Bethlehem, in the land of Judah, are by no means least among the rulers of Judah; for from you shall come a ruler who is to shepherd my people Israel."' Then Herod secretly summoned the wise men and ascertained the exact time the star had appeared. Then he sent them to Bethlehem, saying, 'Go and search thoroughly for the child; and when you find him, report back to me so that I also may pay him homage.'

After listening to the king, they set out; and, sure enough, the star they had seen dawning in the East went ahead of them, until it stopped over the place where the child was. When they saw that the star had stopped, they were beside themselves with joy. Entering the house, they saw the child with Mary his mother, and, prostrating themselves, they paid him homage. Then, opening their treasure chests, they offered him gifts – gold, frankincense and myrrh. Finally, having been warned in a dream not to return to Herod, they returned to their own country by another route.

Meditation

We knew it would be worth it the moment we saw the star,
>worth the hassle,
>the effort,
>the sacrifice,
>but there were times when we wondered, I can tell you!

As we laboured over those dusty barren tracks,
    as we watched fearfully for bandits in the mountains,
    as the sun beat down without a break,
    and still no sign of an end to it,
    we wondered, all too often.
We asked ourselves whether we'd got it wrong,
    misread the signs;
    we argued over whether we'd taken the wrong turning
    somewhere along the way;
    we questioned the wisdom of carrying on as the days dragged by;
    and when, finally, we got to Jerusalem,
    only to find his own people had no idea what was going on,
    then we really became worried.
Quite astonishing – the biggest event in their history,
    and they didn't even realise it was happening!
Thankfully they looked it up,
    eventually,
    somewhere in one of their old prophets,
    and we knew where to go then.
It was all there in writing, if only they'd taken the trouble to look –
    God knows why they couldn't see it!
Anyway, we made it at last,
    tired, sore and hungry,
    but we made it,
    and it was worth it, more than we had ever imagined,
    for in that child was a different sort of king,
    a different sort of kingdom,
    from any we'd ever encountered before –
    as much our ruler as theirs,
    as much our kingdom as anyone's.
So we didn't just present our gifts to him,
    we didn't just make the customary gestures of acknowledgement –
    we fell down and worshipped him.
Can you imagine that?
Grown men –
    respected,

wealthy,
important –
kneeling before a toddler.
Yet it seemed so natural,
    the most natural response we could make,
    the only response that would do!

Prayer

Lord Jesus Christ,
    I rejoice that in you I have found the answer to my searching,
    the one who gives meaning and purpose to life.
Save me, though, from thinking that my journey has ended;
    that I know all there is to know
    and that faith now will take care of itself.
Help me to keep on seeking,
    looking always to grow in grace
    and to know you better.
Teach me that there is more to understand
    and more to experience of your love,
    and so keep me travelling the pilgrim way,
    until finally the journey is over
    and I meet you face to face.
In your name, I ask it.
Amen.

14
Why me?
Mary, the mother of Jesus

The Christmas story, as we have already observed, is one that has captured the imagination of innumerable generations the world over, even those who have no interest in the Christian faith as a whole. Yet, there is a strange irony here. The Christmas narratives are not a story at all but an introduction – the beginnings of a continuing saga that is still being written today. To take a part out of context and focus on that alone is to risk misunderstanding everything it has to say. Nowhere, perhaps, is that more powerfully illustrated than in the experience of Mary. How must she have felt when she learned that she was to bear the Messiah? Well, we have, of course, a fair idea as to that, having focused earlier on her response: 'How can this be, since I am a virgin?' If that, though, was one question, I suspect that she must repeatedly have asked another throughout the course of her pregnancy and at the time of her birth: the simple question, 'Why me?' Why had God chosen her for this honour? Who was she to bear his Son, when there were so many others more eligible? How could she possibly be worthy to bear such a huge responsibility? A question asked in awe and wonder, but, above all, with praise and thanksgiving.

Yet, just thirty-three years later, she must have asked the same question in a very different mood, for now she stood beside a cross watching her son nailed to it – his back lacerated by a Roman whip, his head bleeding from a crown of thorns, his body convulsed in agony as nails were driven into his hands and feet. What had seemed like an honour was fast becoming a nightmare. Why had God chosen her to endure that? Why did she have to experience that most heart-wrenching of sorrows of seeing her own child suffer and die before her very eyes? Which of us, in her place, wouldn't have asked, 'Why me?' Whether she asked it or not, we do not know. Yet, though the truth was probably hidden from her, there was as much cause for rejoicing that day as on the day Jesus was born; in fact more, for this was the moment bringing new birth and new life to all. It was the moment her son had been born for, the supreme expression of God's love for all. There will be times when God has blessed us beyond our imagining and we will ask in wonder, 'Why me?' There will be times when we cry out in despair as life seems fraught with tragedy and sorrow, asking in confusion and even anger, 'Why me?' Sometimes God's purpose is clear, sometimes baffling, yet at the heart of the gospel is the conviction that God is there at all times, and that by his grace, for those who love him, all things will work together for good.

Reading: Luke 2:25-35

There was a man called Simeon in Jerusalem who was upright and devout, eagerly awaiting the consolation of Israel, and the Holy Spirit dwelt upon him. The Spirit had disclosed to him that he would not taste death before he had seen the Lord's Messiah. Led by the Spirit, Simeon entered the temple; and when Jesus' parents brought in their child to honour the customs of the Law, Simeon cradled him in his arms and praised God, saying, 'Master, you are now dismissing your servant in peace, according to your promise. With my own eyes I have seen the salvation you have prepared before all the world – a light that will reveal you to the Gentiles and bring glory to your people Israel.' The child's parents were stunned at these words concerning him. Then Simeon blessed them and said to his mother Mary, 'This child is ordained to be a sign that many will reject; one through whom the inner thoughts of many will be revealed and even your own soul will be pierced. Many in Israel will stand or fall because of him.'

Meditation

Why me?
That's what I kept on asking myself.
Why me?
I mean, it was obvious what people were going to say, wasn't it?
The sly looks,
    the knowing grins,
    the wagging tongues.
And Joseph? Well, he really hit the roof.
Furious he was, and who can blame him?
If we'd been married it would have been different;
    but engaged – it was bound to cause a scandal.
And it hurt, more than anyone will know –
    I never realised people could be so cruel.
I didn't even want a baby, that's what made it worse;
    it was the last thing on my mind.
I was still young,
    not ready for that kind of responsibility,
    wanting to enjoy life a little.
I could have done without those sleepless nights,
    the endless washing,
    the countless extra demands.
And, believe me, it didn't get any easier.
Well, it never does, does it?
I'll never forget how he disappeared like that
    on the way back from Jerusalem;
    a right old panic he had us in.
But was he sorry?
Well, if he was, he had a funny way of showing it.
'You should have known where to find me,' he said –
    'My Father's house, where else?'
Cheeky monkey!
And then, just when life was plodding along nicely,
    back on an even keel,
    he went swanning off into the wilderness to be baptised.

Oh, I know he had to make his own way, don't get me wrong,
    but I couldn't help feeling
    he was getting mixed up in something dangerous.
And so it proved.
We could all see it coming;
    all except him, apparently.
He said the wrong things
    to the wrong people
    in the wrong places,
    and there could only be one result.
It nearly broke my heart to watch it –
    my beautiful boy, broken and bleeding,
    struggling with that cross,
    hanging in agony.
But then he looked down,
    not at the rest of them
    but at me,
    and in his eyes was such love,
    such care,
    such tenderness!
I saw suddenly the eyes of God
    looking at me through the eyes of my child,
    and I asked myself then,
    as I'd asked so many times before,
    yet differently this time,
    so very differently,
    'Why me?
    Why *me*?'

Reading: John 19:25b-26

Mary, the mother of Jesus, and his mother's sister, the wife of Cleopas, and Mary Magdalene, stood by the cross of Jesus. Seeing his mother there, and the disciple whom he loved standing nearby, Jesus said to his mother, 'Woman, behold your son!'

Prayer

Loving God,
 sometimes I cannot help but ask 'Why?'
 'Why me? Why this? Why anything?'
There is so much I do not understand,
 so much that apparently contradicts my faith,
 so much that leaves me groping for answers,
 and all too easily I feel guilty about having such questions,
 afraid that somehow I am letting the side down
 through entertaining them.
Yet, in my heart, I know there is no point pretending,
 for I can never deceive you.
Help me, then, to admit honestly
 that there are things I cannot make sense of,
 and to trust that though *I* may never understand, *you* do.
Amen.

15
The time is coming, they tell me
John Mark, the Evangelist

According to the words of an old saying, 'Much of what we see depends on what we are looking for.' In other words, we often miss something that is staring us in the face, either because we are closed to the possibility of seeing it or because we are preoccupied with something else. Jesus was well aware of the problem; his frequent use of parables and day-to-day illustrations were designed to break through people's preconceptions so that they might see the world in a new light. The need to do that is as real today as it has ever been, and nowhere more so than when it comes to understanding the kingdom of God. All too easily we relegate that kingdom to some far-off place and time, as though it is divorced from daily life, yet nothing could be more wrong. Certainly, the final consummation of God's purpose must come later, but, as Jesus proclaimed at the very start of his ministry, 'The time is fulfilled, and the kingdom of God has come near' (Mark 1:15).

The fact is that the kingdom has already dawned, if only we have eyes to see it. Like yeast or a mustard seed, it is slowly growing, its presence evidenced in countless lives being changed every day, in numerous expressions of love and service, in the work and worship of the Church, and in so much more. The fulfilment may be yet to come, but the kingdom is none the less here among us. As well, then, as looking to the future and praying, 'Come, Lord, come', we need to nurture the seeds that Jesus has already sown, ensuring we do all in our power, through his grace, to see them grow.

Mark 13:32-37

But about that day or hour no one knows, neither the angels in heaven, nor the Son, but only the Father. Beware, keep alert; for you do not know when the time will come. It is like a man going on a journey, when he leaves home and puts his slaves in charge, each with his work, and commands the doorkeeper to be on the watch. Therefore, keep awake – for you do not know when the master of the house will come, in the evening, or at midnight, or at cockcrow, or at dawn, or else he may find you asleep when he comes suddenly. And what I say to you I say to all: Keep awake.

Meditation

The time is coming, they tell me:
    the day of the Lord's return,
    when we shall stand before him
    and he will separate the sheep from the goats,
    the wicked from the righteous;
    so forget about the present,
    think instead of the future,
    for that's what matters –
    our final destiny,
    the life to come –
    nothing else.
Well, I'm sorry, but have I missed something?
For that's not the way I heard it,
    not what I thought Jesus was saying at all.
Keep alert, he warned, certainly,
    for the day will dawn as God has promised,
    but when that will be we've no idea;
    today, tomorrow or far beyond – who can say?
It's not the 'when' of his coming that should concern us,
    but the fact that he will,
    and the difference that makes not to the future
    but to the here and now,

to the way we live every moment of every day.
We've a job to be doing,
    a broken world out there
    needing to hear his word and know his love,
    and that's what will concern him when he comes,
    not whether we've been looking forward eagerly to his kingdom
    but whether we're doing something to make it happen,
    to help build heaven on earth.
So what will he find in you?
A life dedicated to his service,
    continuing his ministry where he left off,
    or an obsession about the future so strong
    that you've forgotten about the present?
A life lived for others,
    committed to bringing light where there is darkness,
    and joy where there is sorrow,
    or a preoccupation with yourself,
    with securing your own salvation?
Don't think I doubt his promise.
The time is coming, just as they say,
    a day when we will be called to account,
    made to answer for the way we've lived our lives.
But if I were you I wouldn't dwell on that too long;
    I'd get down to the business of discipleship,
    to walking the way of the cross,
    or otherwise you may find,
    when the moment comes and judgement is pronounced,
    that the verdict is very different from the one you had in mind.

Prayer

Gracious God,
> you do not want me to see your kingdom
> as a time and a place confined to the distant future;
> you want me to recognise that it is already present
> and, understanding that, to commit myself to helping it grow
> here on earth.

Inspire me through all those who have caught a vision
> of what life can be,
> and who have had the faith and dedication
> to translate that vision into reality.

Help me to learn from them
> and to understand that you are at work in this world,
> striving to fulfil your purpose within all its joy and sorrow,
> beauty and ugliness, good and evil, triumph and tragedy.

Teach me to offer my service, as best I may,
> working with your people everywhere
> to see your will done
> and your kingdom come in all its glory.

Through Christ my Lord.
Amen.